MW01268469

What Has Scales?

Mary Elizabeth Salzmann

Published by ABDO Publishing Company, 8000 West 78th Street, Edina, Minnesota 55439.

Printed in the United States.

Credits
Editor: Pam Price
Content Developer: Nancy Tuminelly
Cover and Interior Design and Production: Mighty Media
Photo Credits: Peter Arnold (Kelvin Aiteken, Courteau Christophe, Roland Seitre), Shutterstock, Steve Wewerka

Library of Congress Cataloging-in-Publication Data

Salzmann, Mary Elizabeth, 1968-

What has scales? / Mary Elizabeth Salzmann.

p. cm. -- (Creature features)

ISBN 978-1-59928-870-3

1. Scales (Fishes)--Juvenile literature. 2. Scales (Reptiles)--Juvenile literature. I. Title.

QL942.S257 2008

591.47'7--dc22

2007004725

Super SandCastle™ books are created by a team of professional educators, reading specialists, and content developers around five essential components–phonemic awareness, phonics, vocabulary, text comprehension, and fluency–to assist young readers as they develop reading skills and strategies and increase their general knowledge. All books are written, reviewed, and leveled for guided reading, early reading intervention, and Accelerated Reader® programs for use in shared, guided, and independent reading and writing activities to support a balanced approach to literacy instruction.

About SUPER SANDCASTLE™

Bigger Books for Emerging Readers

Grades PreK–3

Created for library, classroom, and at-home use, Super SandCastle™ books support and engage young readers as they develop and build literacy skills and will increase their general knowledge about the world around them. Super SandCastle™ books are part of SandCastle™, the leading PreK–3 imprint for emerging and beginning readers. Super SandCastle™ features a larger trim size for more reading fun.

Let Us Know

Super SandCastle™ would like to hear your stories about reading this book. What was your favorite page? Was there something hard that you needed help with? Share the ups and downs of learning to read. We want to hear from you! Send us an e-mail.

sandcastle@abdopublishing.com

Contact us for a complete list of SandCastle™, Super SandCastle™, and other nonfiction and fiction titles from ABDO Publishing Company.

www.abdopublishing.com • 8000 West 78th Street
Edina, MN 55439 • 800-800-1312 • 952-831-1632 fax

Scales are hard, thin plates that cover the bodies of some creatures.

Goldfish have scales.

Goldfish scales come in many colors, including orange, black, red, and white. Some goldfish are multicolored.

Chameleons have scales.

Some chameleons can change the color of their scales to blend into their surroundings.

Moths have scales.

A moth's wings are covered with tiny scales. If you touch a moth's wing, some of the scales may rub off on your finger.

Rattlesnakes have scales.

A rattlesnake's rattle is made of scales that are left each time the snake sheds its skin.

Tortoises have scales.

Tortoises have small scales on their legs and heads. Their shells are made up of large scales called scutes.

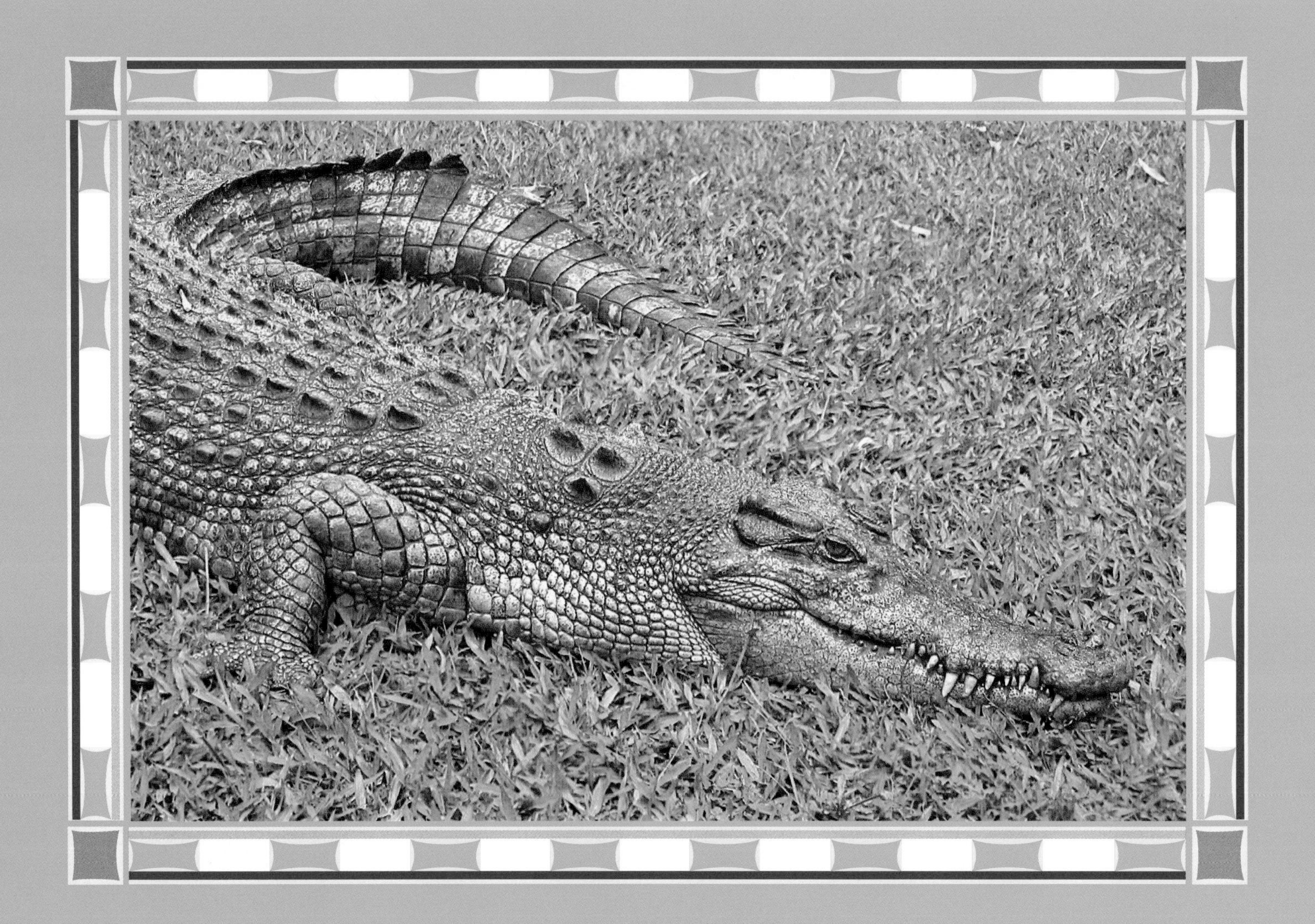

Crocodiles have scales.

Like other reptiles, crocodiles' scales are made of keratin. They have different-sized scales on different parts of their bodies.

Stingrays have scales.

Stingray scales are tiny compared with the scales of most other fish.

Anacondas have scales.

Each yellow anaconda has a unique pattern of yellow and black scales on its underside. The anaconda is the heaviest kind of snake.

Pangolins have scales.

The pangolin defends itself by rolling its body into a tight ball. The hard scales help keep the pangolin from getting hurt.

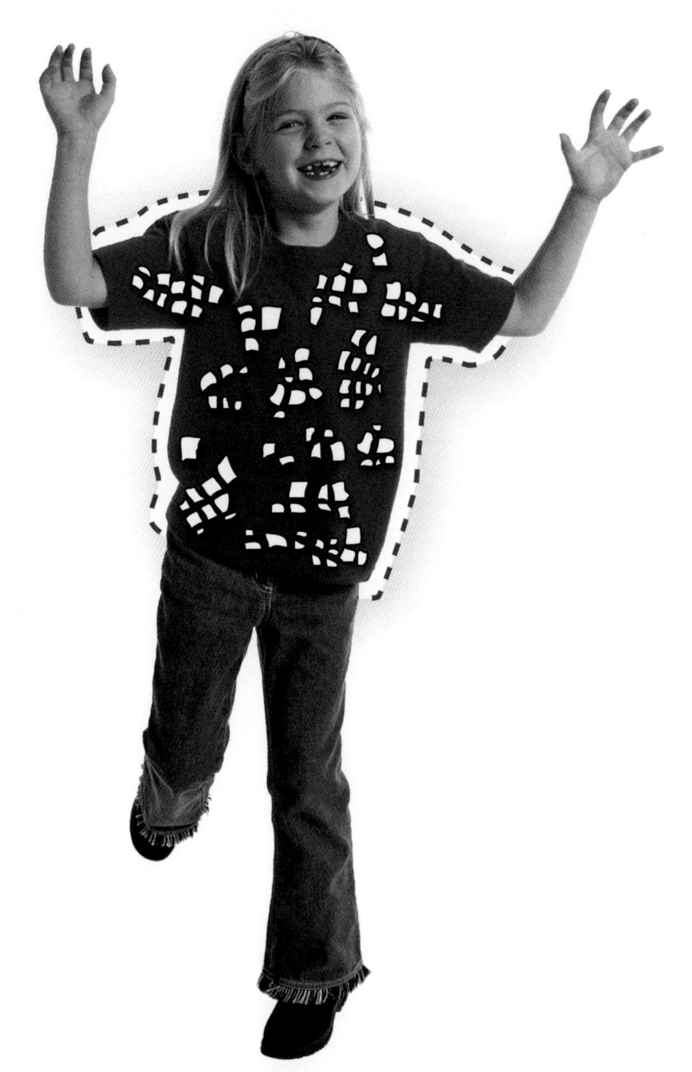

What would you do if you had scales?

MORE CREATURES THAT HAVE SCALES

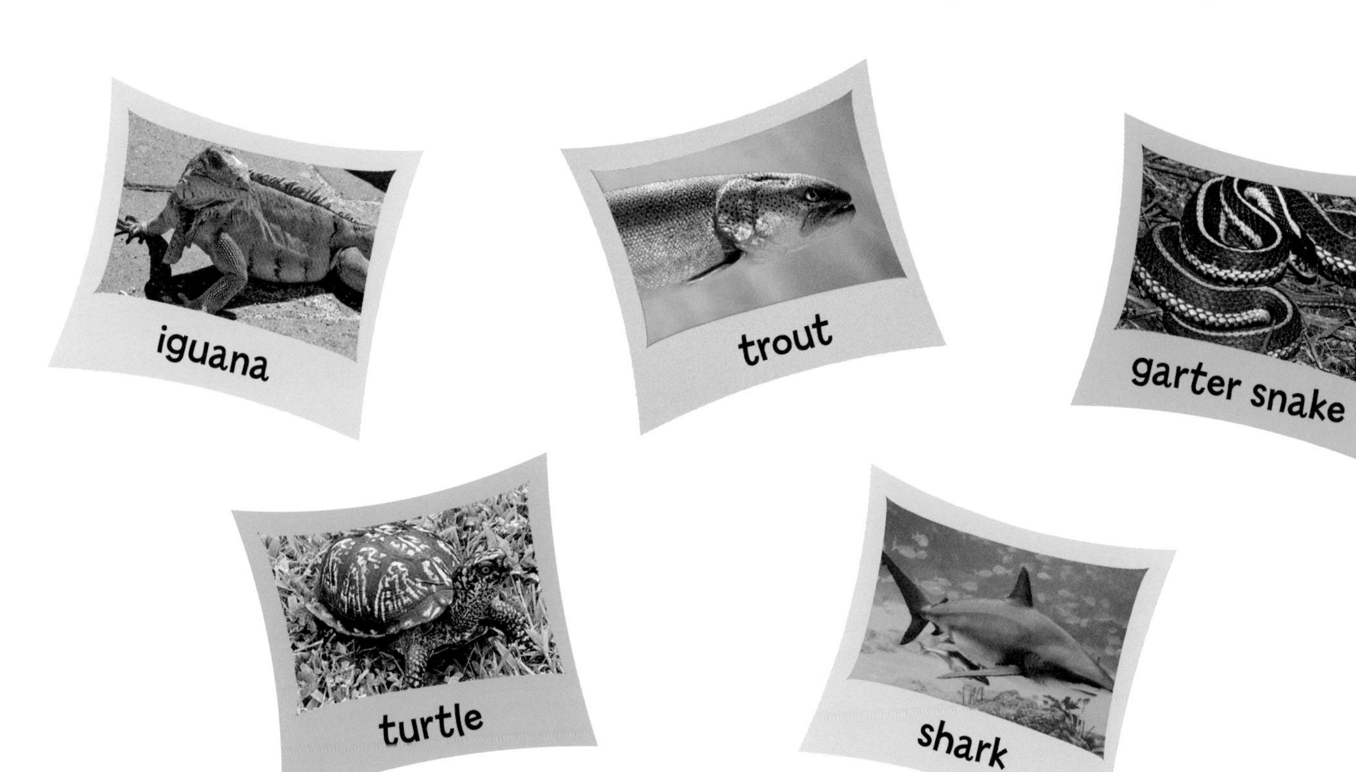

GLOSSARY

blend - to mix things so that you can't tell one from the other.

include - to take in as part of a group.

keratin - a fibrous protein found in hair, feathers, hooves, claws, and horns.

mammal - a warm-blooded animal that is covered with hair and, in the female, produces milk to feed the young.

multicolored - having more than one color.

reptile - a cold-blooded animal, such as a snake, turtle, or alligator, that moves on its belly or on very short legs.

shed - to lose something, such as skin, leaves, or fur, through a natural process.

surroundings - the conditions and things around something or someone.

tongue - the movable muscle in the mouth that is used for tasting and swallowing.

unique - the only one of its kind.